Welcome to your Monday

Beginning of the Week Motivation
in 140 Characters or Less

J CLEVELAND PAYNE

WELCOME TO YOUR MONDAY

iii

J CLEVELAND PAYNE

DEDICATION

This book is dedicated to my always beautiful and usually supportive wife. Thank you for sticking with me for all the good ideas and the least destructive of the bad ideas, even if it is often hard to tell the difference between the two.

J CLEVELAND PAYNE

ACKNOWLEDGMENTS

I first have to thank the real 'inspiration' for the feed and this book, Nikki Woods, Senior Producer for 'The Tom Joyner Morning Show.' One one-off post of so with the opening 'Welcome to your Monday...' sparked the idea that easy to spread a little wisdom, but too short in the amount of words to justify creating another newsletter, at least at the time. I just hope I don't get sued...

I have to follow that with all the friends, family members, co-workers, clients, casual acquaintances, and random people that stumbled upon my work on the internet for reading, responding, and acknowledging this 'alter-ego' work that I had no idea would last two months, let alone almost two years at the time of this writing.

I wrap it up with a quick word of thanks to my parents, John and Pamela Payne. First for putting up with a somewhat frustrating child in me. Most importantly, setting up a home environment where learning was encouraged and meeting new challenges was expected every day.

Welcome to your Monday. That is how I started a tweet in late 2012, followed by 115 more characters. And just like that, I had created another motivational series of sorts, this one a lot shorter than I was used to.

The *Welcome to Your Monday* Twitter series is billed as 'Monday morning motivation in 140 characters or less.' At the time of this writing, it is barely over the year old, and there is no real plan for just how long this series will ultimately live. Just like I am a prolific writer, I am also a *very* prolific project starter, often leaving newsletters and serial piece in limbo. When you start a lot of writing projects in haste, and have a limited amount of time and love to give to those projects, they tend to die in haste as well.

The key to getting this particular project to last this long was the ability of third party Twitter applications to schedule tweet in the future. After a few weeks of posting *Welcome to Your Monday* tweets, I started getting a few ideas at a time, and just wrote and scheduled. I didn't worry about writing masterful paces of insight. I just needed it to fit inside of 140 characters, or even better, 120 characters to allow my username, @jclevelandpayne, to fit in an old school retweet.

To celebrate the ability to, even if by accident, string together a year's worth of these weekly tweets, I wrote expanded commentary for the first 52 and published them in this book. My common disclaimer for any of my motivational / inspirational / get-off-your-butt-and-just-do-something writing is that very little will be found to be original or earthshattering thoughts. While the occasional epiphany is available for you to claim, most of these thoughts and ideas are going to just remind you of what you already should be doing or reaffirm that what you are doing is the right thing. I am *very* okay with that.

If you like what you are reading here, I have plenty more words put down on paper and webpages that I would love for you to check out. You can easily follow me on Twitter to receive more of the *Welcome to Your Monday* tweets (assuming there are still *Welcome to Your Monday* tweets being published) and find a probably outdated list of what I am writing about at my website, jclevelandpayne.net.

WELCOME TO YOUR MONDAY

J CLEVELAND PAYNE

HOW TO READ THIS BOOK

This book contains the first 52 installments of the welcome to you Monday twitter series. Since all tweets began with welcome to your Monday, I will not repeat that phrase 52 times. Consider yourself welcomed to your Monday...or Tuesday...or whatever day of the week you want to read this book.

Each message opens with the original weekly message printed on the left page as it was posted online, in 117 characters or less without the opening salutation. The right page follows with a 2-4 paragraph expanded thought on the main theme of the message.

If you have ever tried, you have probably failed. Failed lately? Learned from that failure? Success is now closer.

Mastering success means you first have to master failure. That phrase has a specific meaning, and it is not the same concept as overcoming failure, which is also a must. Mastering failure begins with becoming comfortable with failure, because following the path to success ensures you will encounter plenty of failure.

The good news is that with every failure, you'll find yourself getting closer to reaching that ultimate success. Each misstep brings you a step closer. The price of success is a sprained knee here' a broken bone there, and plenty of bruises to one's ego. But it is a price that must be paid, and a sacrifice that must be made.

Be prepared to pay. It will be well worth the cost.

Why not try to make it a phenomenal day? Why would you want to try for something other than a phenomenal day?

How you manage your days is up to you. But if you have a finite amount of time to manage, why would you want to waste it by not focusing on making that time as great as possible?

What good is living a life consisting of day after day strung together with no real purpose and even less effort to give any day any purpose? You know tomorrow is coming, and the day after that, and the day after that. Why not work on a habit of starting off with your best foot forward, even if it is impossible to finish on the same note?

In the end, you will only end up with so many days, and will probably not be given the luxury of knowing when your final days are upon you. Don't waste them. Work on them.

You never know who's looking, so always prepared for being positive. Or prepare to explain being negative.

The image you project is the reality that people will accept. Despite all you may do behind closed doors, it is only that you do that can be seen in the public eye that the public will get a chance to judge you on. Fairly or not, it's the public persona that is the real you for all that can't get to know the real you.

Only, you never really know when you are being watched, and by whom. The impressions you make when you think people are not paying attention are powerful, and can show the world more of a 'real you' than you may want to admit to being. That is why it is important to mind your manner in public and private settings.

In this age, anyone can get a digital record of whatever you are doing, and even those most trusted sources can be bought off by the slighted bit of fame for outing you.

Got a few kind words to spare? I'm sure someone could use one or two today. Or every day.

I never really comprehended the true power of words until I began an active effort to use more positive words daily. It is one thing to consider the power of long form writing. It is a totally different animal when you focus on just a few words being directed at particular people.

Actively speaking more positive words and less negative words is not an easy task. It is easy to curse, shout, and complain because there is really so much to curse, shout, and complain about. Asking yourself to refrain from these actions and to create a positive phrase in their place may seem like insanity.

It is not insanity. It may even save your sanity. It will definitely change your perspective on your day for the better, and hopefully lift the spirits of a few others around you.

Success is waiting for you on a higher floor. Take the elevator, or take the stairs. But you can't stand still.

This message takes reaching for success to a literal sense. Your path to success will force you to go vertical, as in take yourself to a higher standard.

To get to where you are going, you will have to leave where you are now. And once you leave, you will change. It is up to you to make that change for the better or allow for that change to make things worse.

Luckily for you, you've chosen to make things better, and that means you've got to step up your game. You've got to climb the ladder of success. Rung by rung, you've got to get higher in order to see the landscape from a better angle.

Inspiration in 140 characters or less isn't as hard as I though. Here it is in 2 characters :)

Actually, inspiration in 140 characters or less is *very* hard. So hard, that I didn't know how many more messages I would tweet out after this one. Luckily, I started getting multiple ideas for messages soon after I posted this one. I knew I really had something, and the ideas just started coming to me.

Just like this one, although it took a lot of cleverness to come up with it at first. A bit of a riddle. Inspiration in two characters became the smiley emoticon, the colon and the parenthesis. The two characters create the image of a sideways smile, and what could be a greater source of inspiration that a simple and sincere smile. Welcome to your Monday. Feel like giving up? Go ahead and quit...doing what isn't working. Start doing anything else and see how it works.

Did anything amazing yet? Well, it's early. Add 'do something amazing' to your to do list.

The Twitter feed is set to automatically tweet at approximately 8:30AM Central time. I write a few at a time and schedule so when they arrive in my feed they are as fresh for me as hey are for you. They are sent to be an early reminder in your day an week.

That is specifically what this tweet is meant to do. Remind you of your duty to attempt something amazing, and if you haven't yet, remind you to add it to you schedule to ensure you don't forget.

There is always something amazing inside of you waiting to be released to the world. The greatest obstacle to you doing amazing things is simply everyday life just getting in the way. Do everything you can to not let that happen. Adding 'do something amazing to your daily to do list helps.

Worried about your future? Do one thing today to ensure something good will happen for some future tomorrow.

In order for you to enjoy the shade of a tree on a hot summer's day, someone needed to plant the tree years in advance. The tree had to grow to a certain level of maturity in order to provide you shade, plus food and shelter for animals.

If you expect to have a future you reap similar benefits, your current you needs to lay the ground work in future you's past. The seeds you sow now will grow into rewards and opportunities that can be harvested years to come. Your legacy can only be secured by the actions you take. Take deliberate action in building a future you can be proud of.

The universe is not conspiring against you. A lack of effort on time management might actually be the culprit.

Despite any evidence you may think you can gather the universe is not conspiring against you. And chances are no living being is plotting your demise either. Well, not living being other that yourself via unconscious thoughts and actions.

Focused and deliberate action is the key to making things happen in your life. Showing up for life looks a lot different than showing up for life on time and prepared to get to work. Chances are if it seems like the stars are aligned to foretell of your potential doom, you should stop looking toward the stars and start looking towards a daily planner. Try you had at a little organization and time management and see how that helps.

Your world is only so big, but the world is much bigger. That means there is always room to expand your world.

One of the harder points to get across to young people is the concept of how big the scope of the world is. Despite wealth or social status, they all can grasp the concept of their world based on the confines of their address and the neighbors living nearby. It's a little more difficult to grasp the concept of the world on a global scale, and how what goes down in their smaller world has greater implications in the big world, and vice versa.

The easiest way to get this message across is to simply begin to expand the young person's world. Take them to a few places they've never been, expose them to people and cultures that are foreign to them. If you have issues with the boundaries of your world versus the whole world, this can work for you as well.

People will screw up, and so will you. If there is no harm and no foul, learn to learn from it and move on. Especially if it is you.

Making mistakes is a simple fact of everyday life. While you do learn what works from successes, you will learn more from seeing what doesn't work in the wake of failure. This works for people who are working for you as well as for you yourself.

In fact, don't think of it as failure. Think of it as a lesson learned and paid for. Learn from the mistakes of others to save your own knowledge for new and unique mistakes. Share the lessons you have learned from those unique mistakes with others so that they can save their knowledge for some new and unique mistakes of their own.

Not living the life you want? Don't let lack be a source of depression. Let possibility motivate you to keep on.

The quickest way to change your fortune is through action. If you are lacking something you need for success, the best course is to take action.

Find out what you are missing. Finding out what you are not missing may even be more important. Formulate a plan of action, and put together everything you need to execute that plan.

Want something bad enough? Don't be afraid to ask for it. But be prepared for a no, and be very prepared for a yes.

What's wrong with asking? The clichéd answer is that the only thing someone can do is tell you no. But there can be just as much fear and apprehension from getting a yes in some cases.

Preparation is the key to help you manage either a yay or nay response. Not receiving permission doesn't mean it not a good idea, but it will definitely be an uncomfortable sell.

A secret known to more than one person will not remain a secret. If you have dirty work to do, do it alone.

There is a growing trend in business of establishing workplaces as no-gossip zones. The old norm of allowing employees to charter around the water cooler , spreading wild inaccuracies about people and operations, is dying. Rumors cannot be controlled, and managers have found the best way to quell rumors it to not allow them to sprout in the first place.

You can take the same approach to letting people know information about yourself that you don't want known by the general populace. You should not let anyone in on your personal business that you cannot trust. If you have any suspicions about trusting people, then you shouldn't trust them.

Even better, you should try to live a life with few skeletons in your closet. With less to hide, you'll have less to worry about. But I'm not one to tell you how to live your life...

The downside to knowing better is that you should do better because of it. Do you? Are you?

The Latin term "ignorantia legis neminem excusat" translates to "ignorance of the law excuses no one," and is the basis for the legal doctrine that ignorance of a law is not an excuse for breaking that law. But where a person with no knowledge of a law can at least argue ignorance, those who know and understand the law have even fewer defenses to excuse away a crime.

We've established that knowledge of better ways offers up not excuse for not following those ways. Yet, too many people find ways to make excuses for their inability to live up to the higher standards they know they should be held to. I am far from immune to this, but constantly struggle to work at doing better, even if there is a legitimate reason causing my lack of action.

So the two questions that wrap up this message. Do you know better? Are you doing better?

Never let your first no be your final answer. Rephrase your questions and try asking a few different people.

An early message dealt how to receive and proceed when you receive no for an answer. Obviously, one way to proceed is to not except that no as a final answer. But it is important to know when your no is really meant to say 'do not proceed' and when it is meant to say 'you are not ready to proceed.'

In fact, the point of confusion may come from the question itself. Start by rephrasing the question, putting new emphasis on the positive outcomes of your actions. If you continue to get answers that are unfavorable to your plan of action, ask other people for their opinion and permission. Be careful if you attempt to go over someone's authority, but don't be afraid to ask around if it could possibly mean finding a new source of support.

The more people you can care less about, the more you can care about yourself. Adjust your ratio accordingly.

In order to have the ability to care for the needs of others, you must first take care of the needs you have yourself. This is the basis for airlines telling you to put on your oxygen mask first in case of cabin depressurization. This is a lesson that I painfully learn firsthand as I neglected caring for my basic health in exchange for getting a few extra daily hours of work done for a few months. Two trips to hospital, four days stuck in a hospital bed each, will wisen you quickly to keeping track of medication.

A way to make caring for yourself easier is to eliminate as many people and problems from your life that you don't have to care. It might sound crass, but you've probably have too many friends and acquaintances you focus on that take much more time and effort than whatever return they provide is worth. I'm sure you believe you have too many projects at work. Find ways to gracefully eliminate some of the excess without causing a similar burden on another.

There is a difference between being good at giving advice and giving good advice. Have you mastered the right one?

Anyone can give advice, and just about everyone does give advice. Unfortunately, all advice given is not created equal. Some advice is helpful, some advice is harmless. Most advice is awful and has the potential to cause a great deal of harm. It is up to the person who receives the advice to determine just how valid that advice really is.

You can lend a hand to those weeding out good and bad advice by looking inward and evaluating where the advice you are giving is coming from. Is it coming for a good place or a bad place? From concern or contempt? From a need to spread more good experiences or to ensure more people share in the misery that you live in?

Too many people have become masters at giving advice (usually uninvited and unwarrented). Too few people know how give good advice and just when it is needed. The latter seem to be the only people who truly understand the difference between being one or the other. I suggest you take a moment to see if you are one of the later examples.

If you are not doing everything possible to reach your goals, admit it. Then start doing more to reach your goals.

It is easy to get so bogged down in the minutia of everyday life that you can easily lose sight of the bigger picture. your bigger picture. Your goals and dreams that you long ago dedicated your life to. what happened? you lost sight of the intended goal, drawn off by some distraction.

What are you going to do about it? first, you're going to admit that you indeed lost your way. then, you're going to rechart your path and start back on it. It's never too late to start again. you just have to make the decision to do it. After you admit to yourself how far off track you truly were.

Can't get your life in gear? Down on your luck? The quickest way to turn it around is to say yes more than no.

When life isn't working in your favor, it is best to evaluate. stop in your tracks and take a look at the path you are taking. the direction that you have been heading in. the landmarks and obstacles that you are leaving behind

take account of the way you answer questions and requests. are you closing more doors by not offering yourself and your kill as you reveal the highway. try accepting more challenges and opting yourself to more possible vulnerability. Try answering more yesses to requests than nos. you'll be pleasantly surprised with the results

Convincing changes what people think. Persuading changes what people do. Master your power of persuasion.

You believe you may know better, and want those you know to know the same. Expecting resistance is normal. Especially if your chosen method of winning over hearts and minds falls under the guise of trying to convince those doing wrong that they are indeed doing wrong. Would you want to listen to a person convinced that you are wrong trying to convince you of the same?

instead, try deploying powers more in line with persuasion as opposed to convincing. It might seem like wordplay, simple semantics, but the implications of persuasion are not as harsh as that of convincing.

We all need a reminder of just how awesome we are. Here is a reminder from me. Plan to send one to yourself.

We do need reminders to let us know that we are awesome, we are doing awesome, and the paths of our lives are destined to be awesome. We need these reminders to come for normally reliable sources, like friends and families. Random reminders from acquaintances and even strangers on the street are great to collect as well.

But the best source of motivation comes in the form of the personal messages you regularly send yourself. That makes the act of scheduling personal messages of your own awesomeness very important. If you can be your harshest critic, you owe it to yourself to also fill the role of your most loyal cheerleader.

Life is harder when you can see both sides of an argument, but views on life are narrower when you can't.

No one is asking you to be cordial to all opinions that oppose your own beliefs. No one is even requesting you have a cliched 'open-minded' when engaging in a heated debate. You are being asked to fight fair, let the other sided finish their statements, and to take a view from the opponent's side. You just don't have to side with them.

Any great debater knows you don't just study all the points that gain favor for your side of the argue, you study the opposing view just as intently. You should have the ability to debate their points for them with as much skill as you debate your own point. This is a chore that forces you to up your game for you own side and find a point where you can respect the person on the opposition, even if you are having a hard time respecting the opposition's cause.

Stop feeling guilty about not getting it all done. If you die today, your inbox will still be full tomorrow.

As a workaholic myself, I am not comfortable not working some point of some project. But I learned pretty early in my adult working life that the time allowed for working per day is limited by the energy you possess in a span of 24 hours. Everyone gets the same 24 hours. Everyone will run out of viable energy in that same 24 hours.

Deadlines and overtimes are great motivators to get your work done. But rarely will you see a day when you can complete everything that needs to be done. It is possible to work yourself to illness and dead, but definitely not worth it. There is always tomorrow to get more work done.

The portion size you can accept depends on the size of your plate. Are you putting too much on a small plate?

This is not a message about maintaining a healthy and nutritious diet, but the analogy fits perfect. This is about maintaining a healthy balance. I had time and energy in mind when I wrote this, but any nagging issue that you could conceive will fit this analogy as well.

Some people have smaller tolerances than other, and try to pull a day made for a person with a much larger plate, and find items spilling over. Some people have larger tolerances than others, and try to slide by on a day made for a person with a much smaller plate, and cannot find themselves fulfilled. This is about knowing your true self and how much you can really handle. Don't play up if it is too much and don't play down if it is too little.

Pains and stress are messages being sent from your body. Your body is tired and needs rest. Listen to your body.

As a certified personal trainer, I have learned that pain is a way to getting a message across. The initial message is 'this body part has been underworked and neglected in the past.' This is easy to decipher and easy to remedy. More work with with plenty of rest in between to build strength and stamina.

As a person with more physical ailment than he ought to have, I also have learned that pain is a way of getting a message across. this message is 'something is wrong...maybe *really wrong*.' Your body can tell you gently or violently when it is in need of a break. You should never let it come to a violent conversation. Take a break when you are tired, rest when you are weary, and get back to hard work after you have taken enough time to recover.

Seeing success? Want to mess with it? The urge can be great, and it is still a bad idea. Don't mess with success.

What do we do when things are going are way? We find a way to sabotage are efforts, of course! One of the greatest threats to massive success it a small mecum of success. This allows for a cloud of doubt to form in your mind which left unchecked, can grow into a storms of self-pity. And crazy as it may sound, small successes are great incubators for grand failures, but people tend to believe they don't deserve the grand success that looks like it's about to come. Hence, self-sabotage.

So what should you do if you are seeing success? Don't mess with it! Study what you are doing to bring success in your life and do everything in your power to keep doing it. Take note of your current circumstances and prepare for any new challenges that could be forming over the horizon, but don't blow up your process or procedures before those challenges arrive on the shore.

Only one player can be the quarterback at a time. If you are not the team lead, focus on your assigned role.

Modern era wrestling fans are very familiar with the catchphrase seized and expanded by superstar Dwayne 'The Rock' Johnson, "Know your role and shut your mouth!" while this message is not focusing on the second part of the phrase, keeping your mouth shut is an important part of the conduct expected in knowing your role.

There are so many roles that must be filled to make an effort an success, but only so many of those roles can be describe as stellar. All are important, but all will not receive grand accolades from droves of adoring fans. For some, this is good thing, as the attention takes always from their ability to get their job done. For others, feeling of jealousy or shame may result in a poorer performance from the lack of attention they believe they deserve. It is very important to know what your actual expectations are, and what the consequences of not living up will mean to the overall effort. And once you accept those expectation, well, you know...

You can only live in this moment, but you must plan your life around future moments, expected or otherwise.

There is no way to live your life in the past. You can live with an old and dead concept of life that you may refuse to relinquish, but you must live in the time frame that is right now. This moment, then the next moment, then the next. Once that moment in time is here, it is instantly gone, never to return.

But that doesn't excuse reckless 'live like there is no tomorrow' behavior. It just enforces the need to live a life based on some sort of plan. I does not have to be a detailed plan, a long term plan, or even a particularly good plan. But a plan is needed.

Waiting for 'someday' to arrive? Today is as good as any to count as someday. Time to get started.

Samuel Beckett's play *Waiting for Godot* has a simple premise of two guys who wait impatiently for a guy who doesn't show, but do nothing to look for him, or even to leave their spot once they agree he's not going to show up. Despite the absurd nature of the characters, it is one of the most beloved of Beckett's plays. It is also a perfect metaphor for how many of us live our lives, waiting for the 'right moment' to arrive to give us the sign we need to act.

The problem is, that right moment doesn't actually exist, unless you call right now the moment you choose. In fact, to use another cliche to prove this point, we go to the famous *Chinese Proverb*, "The best time to plant a tree was 20 years ago. The second best time is now." The conditions will never be perfect for you in whatever endeavor you wish to try you hand. So if you're going to do it, you might as well choose to do it right now.

Have you been asked to do something you didn't want to do? When will you learn you don't have to do it?

Two questions asked. First, have you been asked to do something you didn't want to do? Of course you have. we all have. The second question, when will you learn you don't have to do it? The answer to this question is based on the answer you give to an unasked question, did you do it?

We will all face times where we are asked to do things that we don't want to do that was do because we care for others. Or because we simply have to, regardless of our feelings. Some tasks may even fall into a nebulous job description listing of 'other duties as assigned.' Don't confuse any of these tasks with the monotonous jobs that people want to throw on your back just because they can. Those tasks you don't have to do. so why would you continue to do it?

Important but not getting done? What if a life depended on it? What could keep you from getting it done then?

You always find a way to do what is important to you. You say you need to get to the gym after work, but you have all those TV shows sitting on your DVD that need to be watched. You say you will take some time on Saturday to balance your checkbook and set up a formal budget for next month, but Saturday mornings are for sleeping in and Saturday nights are for going out. I think you can see my point.

As harsh as it is to use, think of the adage of what you would do if your life or the life of someone very dear to you were at risk. Because it ought to be.

Unhappy with an outcome? If you can't overturn it, get over it. Tomorrow is still coming, despite the outcome.

Sometimes you win, sometimes you lose. Sometimes you walk away from your challenger with nothing at all resolved, and nothing that can be done about it. Well, there is one thing that can be done about. You can leave the outcome well enough alone, and walk away from the endeavor. Because there is nothing you can do to change the situation, so you might as well learn to live with it.

The sun will set tonight and rise tomorrow whether you are happy with the result or not. And if it is a result you cannot change, it doesn't matter whether you are happy with the result or not. it is the result that you must move forward with. It is what it it. Do not dwell. Move forward.

Change is a constant thing, and the day you stop changing is the day you begin to die. Are you breathing today?

Every new day is new adventure. Not a chance at new adventure, as truly ne adventure. Every new day is a day that never existed before where you can expect to do things in ways you have never done before, or at least not exactly as you may have done before.

Why ask if you are breathing? If you are breathing, you are obviously physically alive. But any day where you are not prepared to manage change is a day where you are choosing mental regression. You are mentally dying if you're not adjusting to change. Dying mentally always leads to dying physically.

Positive thinking does not guarantee success, but negative thinking is the quickest path to failure.

There is no such thing as a completely sure thing. There is always a chance, even with a probability near infinity, that those infinite odds will be challenged by the worst chance of cosmic luck. So never count on your positive attitude to be the driver of a string of great successes. Although that positive attitude can help.

However, One of the quickest ways to point yourself toward the agony of defeat is to expend your personal energy on negative thinking. Negative though disrupts both your conscious and subconscious mental processes. It literally tunes your focus away from a good outcome. While a good outcome is not impossible, it becomes more and more improbable the longer you stay mire in negative thought.

Positive thinking is only the beginning. Without positive actions, things will never get done. Take action today!

Again, you can never count on your positive attitude to be the driver of a string of great successes. Your attitude is the catalyst to initiate positive actions. Behind enough examples of positive action you will find your potential path to success.

If there is a setup for letdown with this message, it is the fact that you can't stop working. It might look like just a matter of momentum, but it is much more. What is truly at work is the matter of actions.

Any day that you draw breath is a day where anything is possible. What is on your list of possibilities for today?

You have been given a gift today. That gift is another day. Another 24 hours on the planet. This gift is your to do with as you wish because it is, after all, a gift. You can lazily let the day go by and watch another 24 hours turn into history. There aren't too many people whose opinion of what you should do with your new day matter. Plus, not all wasted time is necessarily wasted.

But before warned that this new day, this new set of 24 full hours on this planet, is not renewable. Sure, you could be gifted with another new day tomorrow, but it will not be this particular day, and will not have the particular set of opportunities available. And you are not guaranteed the gift a of a new day tomorrow, so that chance you have to do something special may not come again. You may not have another day to see what possible can occur. Knowing that, know that you should never truly 'waste' a day.

An alarm clock is either a necessity or useless. Determine how much structure you need, not want and prepare for it.

Semantics turns an alarm clock into an 'opportunity' clock, as in it gives you the opportunity to wake up earlier than your sleep cycle may allow so that you can great the world and do great things. I don't like this. I like to think of an alarm clock for what it is, a clock that sounds an alarm to wake you up because you need to get up, despite what your sleep cycle (or bad habit of staying up way to late) are determining you do, stay asleep.

An alarm clock is a real thing for real people who need real structure to help control their lives. If you can wake up at a decent hour without the help of an alarm clock, great! If you can't buy an alarm clock. If you can live you life in free form without much structure and meet all you scheduled appointments, great! If not, put in as much structure in your life as you need to properly function. No more, no less.

Need a reason to be nicer to others? It's the best way to earn the benefit of the doubt, should you need it.

Think of a scenario when you needed the backing of others. It is very easy to come up with a list of propositions that would not work without the support of other people, from the simple and mundane to the elaborate and urgent. It could be a million-dollar proposal or just the destination for an afternoon retreat. But you need other people to see things your way for your way to go forward.

How can you ensure other people see things your way? Well, you cannot but 100% faith in anything, but you can advance the odds significantly in your favor but just being a pleasant person on purpose, but not for the sole purpose of manipulating people at a later date. People like working with people they like. So let people get a chance to like you by generally liking other people.

Bitter pills are not easy to swallow, but improvement means swallowing bitter pills. Get used to it.

You did not enjoy your last feedback session. The words said to you were harsh, bordering on cruel. You are more than a little upset, you are downright angry that an evaluation of you would turn out this way. Even worse, the evaluation was spot on. It was entirely truthful and valid, not the false but glowing report that you would have liked to receive. This does not make you happy.

Guess what? You need to get over it, and yourself. You cannot function at 100 percent 100 percent of the time. You will have some projects miss the mark. You will have some projects wildly miss the mark and go way off course. And proper feedback will help you improve future project. If the proper feedback is a hard to stomach than you should be more worried by the strength of your stomach.

Tomorrow is promised to no one. Have something important to do? Why are you not working on it today?

Procrastination is a personal weakness that I counter with a lot of planning and a few triggering that ensure I am working more than I am putting things off. But beyond the ideas of deadlines and penalties is the reality that we have a limited amount of time on this planet to be able to do things on this planet. Losing key people in my own life showed me this. Having a few personal health scares really got my attention and showed me this.

I might be the only person on this planet who would admit at the moment of death that I wish I would have worked more. I defend this response with a list of the ideas I have been collecting since childhood of things I would like to try, test, and accomplish. The list is already to long to complete in a few lifetimes, but I'm still adding to it. And I am still working toward a futile attempt to complete it. That means every moment gifted to me on this planet is a moment meant for working on something. Even if that something is hugging my wife and kids a few more times before it is all over.

You cannot live for another person. You can choose to live with and/or do for others. You should live for, live with, and do for yourself.

Life is much more fulfilling when you get to share it with other people. It is not so fulfilling when you feel that you have to live your live for other people. The reality is that you do not have to live for anyone other than yourself.

In fact, you have the power to choose who you do want to live with and who you can totally live without. The choices we make and situations that we put ourselves in may make it difficult to divorce ourselves for those people who would choose to completely overtake our lives, but it is still possible.

Are you the average of the people you spend most time with? Or do you bring the average down for groups you enter?

When it comes to personal finances, one of the seemingly overused clichés in the personal development world is the concept that you are the average of the five people you spend most of you time with. While this concept overlaps to all pertinent life skills, it is particularly easily to see the pattern in the relative actions that keep people at their relative standards are living.

If you believe in the concept, you have to believe in order to have an average, you have to have some people who are living exceptionally above the average. You also have to believe that there are some people who are bringing those working at the higher level success down by association. Within your associations, determine where the average line is drawn. Then determine if you are above or below that line. If below, do something about it. If above, do something to help someone below the line raise the average.

If you do something wrong and feel remorse, apologize. If you have not done both, do not. Why waste insincere words?

I personally hate being told I have to apologize. I don't hate apologizing if I am in the wrong, because in those cases I am compelled by my spirit to apologize. But I truly hate being told I have to apologize, because it means I don't think I'm in the wrong, and I am being force to save face for someone else.

I also hate insincere apologies I receive from other people. I rather have no apology from a person I disagree with if they do not feel like they are in the wrong, because I'm not going to apologize to that person if I were in the same situation. Unless I am forced. Which does happen more than it should when you work in the idea's business. But I don't like it.

Ask yourself, "Who do you think you are?" When your answer can convince yourself, your answer will convince anyone.

How well do you think you know yourself? It is an important to ask what you 'think' you know of yourself because too often, we let other people's definitions of what they think we should be live as the definitions we take on for ourselves. And even if we do not let others put a definite definition on us, we choose to not put a definite definition of ourselves on ourselves either. Mostly for fear of being forced to explain or defend that definition.

Why fear this test? Why not take pride in who you are, and most importantly, who you are not. If asked, 'Who do you think you are,' you are the only person with the right answer to the query. You just have to be confident while giving the honest answer. Don't know the answer? Okay, you need to do a little homework to find the answer.

Lessons are learned best when you do not take the good advice you know you should. Sound about right?

Everyone you know will have an opinion of what you should do in your situation. Everyone can offer you some advice on how to handle it. Some of it will not truly fit your situation. Some of it will not fit your personality or demeanor. Some of it will just be plain bad advice. But some of it will be valid and possibly useful good advice. And you will choose to follow the first three types over the last type more often than not.

Why do we pass on taking good advice, even when we know we should? In our minds, we always think we know what is best for us. Some situations don't allow for us to truly see the landscape, and the sound advice we think we don't need gets pushed to the back of our minds. It's good advice, but we don't need it because we think we can do fine on our own. And it comes back to haunt us as a lesson learned as soon as we come to our senses and take the good advice.

Some days are harder to count blessings than others. Those days are most important for counting blessings.

Every day you get to spend on the top side of the top soil is a blessing, but living through the realities of some days can seem like a nightmare. We all have problems that can be compounded to ridiculous proportions at a moment's notice. No one is immune to the occasion day, or occasional string of bad days together.

You know what works best on a bad day? A good memory! Because the days when bad things are happening all around you are the best days to appreciate the good things that have pasted, and the potential great things to come. This day may not seem like a blessing now, but at a later date even the hard times can be seen as a fonder time.

The answers to your questions are always loud and clear. The source of your answers may surprise you.

An unofficial inspiration for the 'Welcome To Your Monday' feed is my old 'You Already Have The Answers' newsletter. The message behind this weekly advice column was that the answers are always there, it's just a matter of asking the right questions. I totally stand by this belief.

I always believed that the answers to all your questions are not only available, but readily accessible to anyone willing to take them in. But where do the answers come from? Most of them are alive in your head just ready for you to listen for yourself. The fact that you are the prime source for just about every answer that you seek is a scenario that many are unable to accept.

History has only recorded one perfect person. That person is neither you nor I. Don't be so hard on yourself.

This was a controversial message. Partly because of the source of the original quote (a speaker for a now defunct personal improvement seminar circuit) and for the implication of a 'perfect person' itself. The 'Welcome To Your Monday' messages are rarely spiritual or religious, but this one is a little of both, and I did receive some angry feedback because of what is implied that I am 'selling.' For the record, I don't go around selling my faith and religious beliefs, I sell services and information that is backed in part by my faith and religious beliefs. They can't be separated, but they are not prominently advertised. On purpose.

Society can debate the true level of perfection that that certain person may or may not have possessed, but the fact remains that you are not that person. Regardless of what religion you want to claim or dispel, you are not a perfect person, so you should not be so hard on yourself when you prove as such.

Conversations where everyone says the same thing get boring fast. Try to share ideas with someone you disagree with.

I spent a great deal of time debating my 'perfect person' message with a guy I consider a good friend and a super intelligent fellow. He just happens to be a very vocal proponent of organized religion. He also roots for a rival NFL teams. There are plenty of subjects we can more or less agree on, but religion and football do not fall into those categories. And that is why I love talking religion and football with him.

Neither one of us expect to change the other's mind on those hot button topics, but we always offer intelligent and respectful debate when we bring them up (and we have plenty of other more cordial conversation topics that we engage in as well). Because it is interesting conversation, not a echo chamber conversation that can be had with drones that blindly support all of your favorite causes.

Don't stop offering help. The people that need your help the most are least likely to believe so, or accept.

For some people, accepting help is a frustrating and difficult task. I should know, because I have a problem with accepting help that is wrap in a lot of different weird mental 'things' that are shuffling in my head. But I know I need help in just about everything I want to accomplish, so I accept it. Sometimes with a mumble or a whimper, but I accept sincere assistance whenever it I offered to me.

And you should offer sincere assistance whenever you can to people you deem worthy, even if they don't deem themselves as worthy. The people who can use your help the most are the least likely to ask for it, and will be reluctant to accept it, regardless of your motives. That's not excuse to stop attempting to offer help. It may surprise you just how much you need to assist as they may need the assistance.

Your future is shaped by your past, but should not look like your past. Look forward, move forward, live forward.

Think our your past as the blueprint from which your current self has been build, and a road map to suggest the direction that you future self will travel. You present and future self we're dependent on your past (good, bad or indifferent) for shaping who you are and what you are to be. But that won't impede your ability to change the course mapped out in your past to adjust you present you and completely change the direction the future you will eventual travel.

You don't go backwards on the path on a map just because. It will delay you getting to the big 'x' that marks your destination. Keep looking forward and working for forward progress. Consult the map of your path occasionally to gauge how far you have traveled and where your destination began. Always know that your final destination is about where you end up, not where you came from.

ABOUT THE AUTHOR

J Cleveland Payne is a marketing and promotions consultant based out of Little Rock, Arkansas. He is the driving force behind Fast Forward Business Properties, LLC, a business and media consulting firm that specializes in helping small business and individual craft their message and master its delivery to the world. He likes to think of himself as 'America's Next Great Radio Talk Show Host,' even if no one else is willing to go along with that description. Payne offers commentary on news and current events, along with advice on personal and professional development to just about anybody that will listen.

You can read more words from Payne by visiting JClevelandPayne.net and email him your own words at jclevelandpayne@gmail.com.

J CLEVELAND PAYNE

WELCOME TO YOUR MONDAY

Made in the USA
Charleston, SC
07 October 2014